DON PATERSON

Rain

Don Paterson has written four previous collections of poems: *Nil Nil*, *God's Gift to Women*, *The Eyes*, and *Landing Light*, which won both the T. S. Eliot Prize and the Whitbread Prize for Poetry. He lives in Kirriemuir, Angus, Scotland.

Also by Don Paterson

Poetry
NIL NIL
GOD'S GIFT TO WOMEN
THE EYES
LANDING LIGHT
ORPHEUS

Aphorism
THE BOOK OF SHADOWS
THE BLIND EYE
BEST THOUGHT, WORST THOUGHT

As Editor
IOI SONNETS
ROBERT BURNS: SELECTED POEMS
DON'T ASK ME WHAT I MEAN (with Clare Brown)
NEW BRITISH POETRY (with Charles Simic)

Rain

Rain

DON PATERSON

Farrar, Straus and Giroux

New York

Farrar, Straus and Giroux
18 West 18th Street, New York 10011

Distributed in Canada by D&M Publishers, Inc.
Printed in the United States of America
Originally published in 2009 by Faber and Faber Ltd, Great Britain
Published in 2010 in the United States by Farrar, Straus and Giroux
First American paperback edition, 2011

Library of Congress Control Number: 2009938696
Hardcover ISBN: 978-0-374-24629-7
Paperback ISBN: 978-0-374-53268-0

www.fsgbooks.com

1   3   5   7   9   10   8   6   4   2

i.m. Michael Donaghy

*Man is air in the air and in order to become
a point in the air he has to fall.*

– Antonio Porchia

Acknowledgements

Acknowledgements are due to the editors of the following publications: *The Book of St Andrews, Brick, Granta, Lights off the Quay, London Review of Books, The New Yorker, Poetry, Poetry Review*. An early version of 'Phantom' appeared in the exhibition catalogue for Alison Watt's *Phantom*, published by the National Gallery, London.

Contents

Rain

Two Trees

One morning, Don Miguel got out of bed
with one idea rooted in his head:
to graft his orange to his lemon tree.
It took him the whole day to work them free,
lay open their sides, and lash them tight.
For twelve months, from the shame or from the fright
they put forth nothing; but one day there appeared
two lights in the dark leaves. Over the years
the limbs would get themselves so tangled up
each bough looked like it gave a double crop,
and not one kid in the village didn't know
the magic tree in Miguel's patio.

The man who bought the house had had no dream
so who can say what dark malicious whim
led him to take his axe and split the bole
along its fused seam, then dig two holes.
And no, they did not die from solitude;
nor did their branches bear a sterile fruit;
nor did their unhealed flanks weep every spring
for those four yards that lost them everything,
as each strained on its shackled root to face
the other's empty, intricate embrace.
They were trees, and trees don't weep or ache or shout.
And trees are all this poem is about.

The Error

As the bird is to the air
and the whale is to the sea
so man is to his dream.

His world is just the glare
of the world's utility
returned by his eye-beam.

Each self-reflecting mind
is in this manner destined
to forget its element,

and this is why we find
however deep we listen
that the skies are silent.

For Once

to give so little insult to the air
it might forgive the earlier disgrace
and leave no sign that I was ever there

as a wanted man might slip over the border
and, believed at last, live out his days
hidden by a silent holy order.

The Swing

The swing was picked up for the boys,
for the here-and-here-to-stay
and only she knew why it was
I dug so solemnly

I spread the feet two yards apart
and hammered down the pegs
filled up the holes and stamped the dirt
around its skinny legs

I hung the rope up in the air
and fixed the yellow seat
then stood back that I might admire
my handiwork complete

and saw within its frail trapeze
the child that would not come
of what we knew had two more days
before we sent it home

I know that there is nothing here
no venue and no host
but the honest fulcrum of the hour
that engineers our ghost

the bright sweep of its radar-arc
is all the human dream
handing us from dark to dark
like a rope over a stream

But for all the coldness of my creed
for all those I denied
for all the others she had freed
like arrows from her side

for all the child was barely here
and for all that we were over
I could not weigh the ghosts we are
against those we deliver

I gave the empty seat a push
and nothing made a sound
and swung between two skies to brush
her feet upon the ground

The Handspring

How me of me, I know, to blame it all
on that little hampered run, that running tiptoe

and the whole world swung up on your fingertips
as if it were nothing, or at least the weight of nothing.

Why Do You Stay Up So Late?
for Russ

I'll tell you, if you really want to know:
remember that day you lost two years ago
at the rockpool where you sat and played the jeweller
with all those stones you'd stolen from the shore?
Most of them went dark and nothing more,
but sometimes one would blink the secret colour
it had locked up somewhere in its stony sleep.
This is how you knew the ones to keep.

So I collect the dull things of the day
in which I see some possibility
but which are dead and which have the surprise
I don't know, and I've no pool to help me tell –
so I look at them and look at them until
one thing makes a mirror in my eyes
then I paint it with the tear to make it bright.
This is why I sit up through the night.

The Circle
for Jamie

My boy is painting outer space,
and steadies his brush-tip to trace
the comets, planets, moon and sun
and all the circuitry they run

in one great heavenly design.
But when he tries to close the line
he draws around his upturned cup,
his hand shakes, and he screws it up.

The shake's as old as he is, all
(thank god) his body can recall
of that hour when, one inch from home,
we couldn't get the air to him;

and though today he's all the earth
and sky for breathing-space and breath
the whole damn troposphere can't cure
the flutter in his signature.

But Jamie, nothing's what we meant.
The dream is taxed. We all resent
the quarter bled off by the dark
between the bowstring and the mark

and trust to Krishna or to fate
to keep our arrows halfway straight.
But the target also draws our aim –
our will and nature's are the same;

we are its living word, and not
a book it wrote and then forgot,
its fourteen-billion-year-old song
inscribed in both our right and wrong –

so even when you rage and moan
and bring your fist down like a stone
on your spoiled work and useless kit,
you just can't help but broadcast it:

look at the little avatar
of your muddy water-jar
filling with the perfect ring
singing under everything.

The Rain at Sea

Aye, maybe I did resent
your home in every element.
But did you know, when you were one

with the dance or dive or ride or run
and lost to water, earth or air
how lost you were to me? Or care?

Let me tell you how it was.
We'd stopped four miles outside Montrose
to let the southbound train slip by.

It was evening, and the sea and sky
were one blue flag, with no design
but for the darker bluer line

where the upper rested on the lower,
and one small cloud ten miles offshore.
The cloud had drawn up to a halt

to leave the sea a gram less salt.
It poured down on no rock or ship
but just upon its own dark shape,

combing out its rain like wool,
like a girl her hair above a pool;
or else (all I could do was sit

before the scene, and worry it)
the sea reached up invisibly
to milk the ache out of the sky.

While I was reckoning the strange
intimate far-off exchange,
the feeling took an age to name.

It was an awful creeping shame.
Nothing on earth was ever less
concern of mine than that caress,

if such a human word would do
for what I saw; and worse, I knew
the whole sea fixed me in its stare.

How did I blunder into here?
There would be all hell to pay.
I turned and shut my eyes and lay

my head against the growling glass
and waited for the train to pass.

The Human Sheld

The reason, gin ye waant the truth,
I sleep like this – ma gairdie stieve
upon yer breist, its steekit nieve
laid on yer sma' hert like an aith –

is no' for waarmth or peace o' mind
but that in ma dreams, ma dou,
I'm staunin here upricht, wi' you
the lang sheld that I grue ahind.

gin: if; *gairdie*: forearm; *stieve*: firm, steady; *steekit*: stiff;
nieve: fist; *aith*: oath; *dou*: dove; *grue*: shudder

The Lie

As was my custom, I'd risen a full hour
before the house had woken to make sure
that everything was in order with The Lie,
his drip changed and his shackles all secure.

I was by then so practised in this chore
I'd counted maybe thirteen years or more
since last I'd felt the urge to meet his eye.
Such, I liked to think, was our rapport.

I was at full stretch to test some ligature
when I must have caught a ragged thread, and tore
his gag away; though as he made no cry,
I kept on with my checking as before.

Why do you call me The Lie? he said. I swore:
it was a child's voice. I looked up from the floor.
The dark had turned his eyes to milk and sky
and his arms and legs were all one scarlet sore.

He was a boy of maybe three or four.
His straps and chains were all the things he wore.
Knowing I could make him no reply
I took the gag before he could say more

and put it back as tight as it would tie
and locked the door and locked the door and locked the door

Correctives

The shudder in my son's left hand
he cures with one touch from his right,
two fingertips laid feather-light
to still his pen. He understands

the whole man must be his own brother
for no man is himself alone;
though some of us have never known
the one hand's kindness to the other.

Song for Natalie 'Tusja' Beridze

O Natalie, O TBA, O Tusja: I had long assumed the
terrorist's balaclava that you sport on the cover of *Annulé* –
which was, for too long, the only image of you I
possessed – was there to conceal some ugliness or deformity
    or perhaps merely spoke (and here, I hoped against
hope) of a young woman struggling
    with a crippling shyness. How richly this latter theory
has been confirmed by my Googling!

    O who is this dark angel with her unruly Slavic
eyebrows ranged like two duelling pistols, lightly sweating
in the pale light of the TTF screen?
    O behold her shaded, infolded concentration, her
heartbreakingly beautiful face so clearly betraying the true
focus of one not merely content – as, no doubt, were others
at the Manöver Elektronische Festival in Wien –
    to hit *play* while making some fraudulent correction to a
volume slider
    but instead deep in the manipulation of some complex
real-time software, such as Ableton Live, MAX/MSP or
Supercollider.

    O Natalie, how can I pay tribute to your infinitely
versatile blend of Nancarrow, Mille Plateaux, Venetian
Snares, Xenakis, Boards of Canada and Nobukazu Takemura
    to say nothing of those radiant pads – so strongly
reminiscent of the mid-century bitonal pastoral of Charles
Koechlin in their harmonic bravura –
    or your fine vocals, which, while admittedly limited in
range and force, are nonetheless so much more affecting

than the affected Arctic whisperings of those
interchangeably dreary
   Stinas and Hannes and Björks, being in fact far closer in
spirit to a kind of glitch-hop Blossom Dearie?

   I have also deduced from your staggeringly ingenious
employment of some pretty basic wavetables
   that unlike many of your East European counterparts, all
your VST plug-ins, while not perhaps the best available
   probably all have a legitimate upgrade path – indeed I
imagine your entire DAW as pure as the driven snow, and not
in any way buggy or virusy
   which makes me love you more, demonstrating as it does
an excess of virtue given your country's well-known talent
for software piracy.

   Though I should confess that at times I find your habit of
maxxing
   the range with those bat-scaring ring-modulated
sine-bursts and the more distressing psychoacoustic properties
of phase inversion in the sub-bass frequencies somewhat taxing
   you are nonetheless as beautiful as the mighty Boards
themselves in your shameless organicising of the code,
   as if you had mined those saws and squares and ramps
straight from the Georgian motherlode.

   O Natalie – I forgive you everything, even your
catastrophic adaptation of those lines from 'Dylan's' already
shite
   Do Not Go Gentle Into That Good Night

in the otherwise magnificent 'Sleepwalkers', and when
you open up those low-
	pass filters in what sounds like a Minimoog emulation
they seem to open in my heart also.

O Natalie: know that I do not, repeat, do *not* imagine
you with a reconditioned laptop bought with a small grant
from the local arts cooperative in the cramped back bedroom
of an ex-communist apartment block in Tbilisi or Kutaisi
	but at the time of writing your biographical details are
extremely hazy;
	however, I feel sure that by the time this poem sees the
light of day Wire magazine will have honoured you with a
far more extensive profile than you last merited when
mention of that wonderful Pharrell remix
	was sandwiched between longer pieces on the notorious
Kyoto-based noise guitarist Idiot O'Clock, and a woman
called Sonic Pleasure who plays the housebricks.

However this little I have gleaned: firstly, that you are
married to Thomas Brinkmann, whose records are boring –
an opinion I held long before love carried me away –
	and secondly, that TBA
	is not an acronym, as I had first assumed, but Georgian
for 'lake' – in which case it probably has a silent 't', like
'Tbilisi', and so is pronounced *baa*
	which serendipitously rhymes a bit with my only other
word of Georgian, being your term for 'mother' which is
'dada', or possibly 'father' which is 'mama'.

I doubt we will ever meet, unless this somehow reaches
you on the wind;
we will never sit with a glass of tea in your local
wood-lined café while I close-question you on how you
programmed that unbelievably great snare on 'Wind',
of such brickwalled yet elastic snap it sounded exactly
like a 12" plastic ruler bent back and released with great
violence on the soft gong
of a large white arse, if not one white for long.

But Natalie – Tusja, if I may – I will not pretend I hold
much hope for us, although I have, I confess, worked up my
little apologia:
I am not like those other middle-agey I-
DM enthusiasts: I have none of their hangdog pathos,
my geekery is the dirty secret that it should be
and what I lack in hair, muscle-tone and rugged good
looks I make up for with a dry and ready wit . . . but I know
that time and space conspire against me.

At least, my dear, let me wish you the specific best:
may you be blessed
with the wonderful instrument you deserve, fitted –
at the time of writing – with a 2 GHz dual-core Intel chip
and enough double-pumped DDR2 RAM for the most
CPU-intensive processes;
then no longer will all those gorgeous acoustic spaces

be accessible only via an offline procedure involving a freeware convolution reverb and an imperfectly recorded impulse response of the Concertgebouw made illegally with a hastily-erected stereo pair and an exploded crisp bag

for I would have all your plug-ins run in real-time, in the blameless zero-latency heaven of the 32-bit floating-point environment, with no buffer-glitch or freeze or dropout or lag;

I would also grant you a golden midi controller, of such responsiveness, smoothness of automation, travel and increment

that you would think it a transparent intercessor, a mere copula, and feel machine and animal suddenly blent.

This I wish you as I leave Inverkeithing and Fife

listening to *Trepa N* for the two hundred and thirty-fourth time in my life

with every hair on my right arm rising in non-fascistic one-armed salutation

towards Natalie, Tba, my Tusja, and all the mountain lakes of her small nation.

Renku: My Last Thirty-five Deaths

I

Blossom-snow.
By noon the pear tree stands
in its white shadow.

II

Just before I left the race
the old moon lost its human face

III

Aha! The zip
for that idiot-suit.
And inside? Zip!

IV

Just let me add my two cents' worth
to the dead weight of the earth

V

'*Every* night
is our last night,' he'd say.
No. Not quite.

VI

Nothing stirs the old millpond.
The frog slips in without a sound.

VII

It wasn't death
fogging the window;
it was my breath

VIII

If I had had a happier dream
this might have been a better poem

IX

Get my *koto*:
its open strings have all
the tunes I know

X

Here's your book back, world. Good story.
I underlined a few things. Sorry.

XI

Maw? Mibbe best
Ah bide aff skale the day
it's ma chest

XII

Sing me that old silent song.
That's the one. It's been so long.

XIII

Attribute
this blank look not to shutdown
but reboot

XIV

Repeat, now: *nought plus one is all;*
but all less one, nothing at all.

XV

Born man, die god.
What hell would fashion
such a fraud?

XVI

The walls fly off, the ceilings, floors . . .
I wish I'd known we'd been indoors

XVII

My puppeteer:
seems he forgot he had
to be somewhere

XVIII

Just then I heard my mother chide
no more TV – go play outside!

XIX

At last, quiet heart.
Eighty years we waited
for one spare part

XX

For years I watched the blossom fall.
It didn't. I rose through it all.

XXI

The hydrangea
starts green; ends green; so why
the changer?

XXII

The cloud above the lake sinks down
to kiss its twin; then both are gone.

XXIII

Why are you crying?
Honestly, you'd think
someone was dying

XXIV

At least I leave the world I lost
an ounce more real for one less ghost

XXV

Say: *he'd the look*
of a fly between the pages
of a closing book

XXVI

My skull clear of all how and why
but this, the last cloud in the sky

XXVII

'What am I *thinking?*'?
Look: this is hardly the time
to quit drinking

XXVIII

As the wind a leaf across the floor,
so time moved me. Now close the door.

XXIX

Listen to this –
I finally found a cure
for my tinnitus

XXX

I came to pass; I came to pass.
I went like frost upon the grass.

XXXI

You need a slapping . . .
I'm not myself? Yeah, well –
The mask is slipping

XXXII

All my life, the moon kept pace.
Tonight I guess I won the race.

XXXIII

I know the deal,
but I've nothing ready! – uh . . .
it's been real

XXXIV

Downcast? Me? I'm overjoyed –
it's my birthday in the Void

XXXV

Give me an hour,
then look in the birdsong, her eye-star,
the spring shower

XXXVI

Too late to blame, too soon to thank –
this page intentionally left blank

Unfold
i.m. Akira Yoshizawa

The Bathysphere

What would you want with that? they said, and fairly,
when the auctioneer's van dumped it in the drive.
It was far worse than they knew. One absent bidder
had ruined me for the thing, the quartz was cracked

and I'd lied about it being a prototype.
None survived, thanks to the famous flaw
that left them on the seabed with their pilots
smeared all over their one wall. No matter –

this thing still looked straight out of the codex
with its double skin of pig iron and sheet steel,
the daft bespoke of all that brass-and-walnut
and, of course, that eye. Which I avoided.

From the air I must have looked like a dung-beetle
as I wrestled it, all breathers and reverses,
over the hill and into the ring of rocks
I'd laid the day before as anchorage.

What *did* I want with it? God only knows
there were days when I wondered, sat bored to tears
with my legs asleep, my hands on the dead levers
and barely light to read the empty log,

but something – it was maybe just the cost –
had me stay on, and so I kept my station
till such goose-cries or gear-grinds as could reach me
came slowed and lowered as through a dream of water.

Two years into my watch they showed themselves.
Shadows too fast for clouds, too slow for birds;
then a looming black-eyed face I thought
some kid's, until I saw it had no mouth.

Now work was a pure joy. I tuned and attuned
and saw their shapes darken and clarify
and heard the bell fill up with their long song.
I was happy. I mean: it would have been enough.

It was the morning. I heard a chain lock up
on the roof, the rocks grind under me
and before I understood the meaning of it
we came free, and a great force bore us upward.

How long the raising took I do not know
but through the weightless orb there rang a song
so vast and strange I thought my head would burst.
My eardrums did. I was so long past caring

that when the quarry clanged under the bowl
where I lay curled, I had to prompt myself
to be bewildered. In that hourless day
my only certainty was that we'd risen.

It took me both my hands to turn the wheel.
Light cut the door; I put my weight to it
and took my small step down into a world
that was identical and wholly other.

When they ask me what I saw, they all expect
some blissed-out excuse for my not saying,
but I know what I saw: I saw in everything
the germ and genius of its own ascent,

the fire of its increase; I saw the earth
put forth the trees, like a woman her dark hair;
I saw the sun's star and the river's river,
I saw the whole abundant overflow;

I saw my own mind surge into the world
and close it all inside one human tear;
I saw how every man-made thing will turn
its lonely face up to us like a child's;

I saw that time is love, and time requires
of everything its full expenditure
that love might be conserved; and then I saw
that love is not what we mean by the word.

For some idea of it, choose a point
in the middle of a waterfall, and stare
for as long as you can stand. Now look around:
see how every rock and tree flows upwards?

So the whole world blooms continually
within its true and hidden element,
a sea, a beautiful and lucid sea
through which it pilots, rising without end.

The Story of the Blue Flower

My boy was miles away, yes, I admit it,
but the place was empty, my lines of sight were good
and besides, such things were unknown in this town –
though none of this did much to comfort me
when I raised my head to see the two of them
stop his mouth and lift him from the swing
with a kind of goblin-like economy
and hurry off his little flexing torso
to the orange van laid up behind the gate.
And that was that. I knew it was all over.

I was in the northeast corner of the park,
waist-deep in the ferns where I'd been hunting
the small black ball we'd lost the day before.
I howled, of course I did, but nothing came.
I only knew that failure of the will
as when you wake inside your sleeping body
and find you have no choice but to fall back
to your dead dream again. And so I did.
I fell to somewhere far below the earth
beside the roar of blind and nameless rivers.

Night followed night. I'd been a lifetime there
when through the dark I saw a pale blue star
I half-recalled, like a detail from a book
I'd loved and feared as a child. Then weeds, and sky
and all was bright and terrible again
except that I was fixed on the blue flower,
like one of those they say are always with us
whose silent glamour makes invisible.
Either way, I was suddenly on my knees
filling and filling my mouth with its bad leaves.

I can call back nothing of the missing hours
but vague things, between image and sensation:
a black wind, a white knife in my head,
and an awful centrifugal déjà vu
slowly slowing to the place I knew
as home, and the boy safe, and the boy safe.
They found them wandering the park at dusk
crying like two wee birds, their crimson faces
streaming with the jellies of their eyes
and no story they could tell of anything.

Parallax

the unbearable lightness of being no one
— Slavoj Žižek

The moon lay silent on the sea
as on a polished shelf
rolling out and rolling out
its white path to the self

But while I stood illumined
like a man in his own book
I knew I was encircled by
the blindspot of its look

Because the long pole of my gaze
was all that made it turn
I was the only thing on earth
the moon could not discern

At such unearthly distance
we are better overheard.
The moon was in my mouth. It said
A million eyes. One word

for Michael Longley

Motive

If we had never left this room
the wind would be a ghost to us.
We wouldn't know to read the storm
into the havoc in the glass

but only see each bough and leaf
driven by its own blind will:
the tree, a woman mad with grief,
the bush, a panicked silver shoal.

Something hurries on its course
outside every human head
and no one knows its shape or force
but the unborn and the dead;

so for all that we are one machine
ploughing through the sea and gale
I know your impulse and design
no better than the keel the sail –

when you lift your hand or tongue
what is it moves to make you move?
What hurricanes light you along,
O my fire-born, time-thrown love?

The Day

for Maureen and Gus

Life is no miracle. Its sparks flare up
invisibly across the night. The heart
kicks off again where any rock can cup
some heat and wet and hold it to its star.
We are not chosen, just too far apart
to know ourselves the commonplace we are,

as precious only as the gold in the sea:
nowhere and everywhere. So be assured
that even in our own small galaxy
there is another town whose today-light
won't reach a night of ours till Kirriemuir
is nothing but a vein of hematite

where right now, two – say hairless, tall and dark,
but still as like ourselves as makes no odds –
push their wheeled contraptions through the park
under the red-leafed trees and the white birds.
Last week, while sceptic of their laws and gods
they made them witness to their given word.

They talk, as we do now, of the Divide;
but figure that who else should think of this
might also find some warmth there, and decide
to set apart one minute of the day
to dream across the parsecs, the abyss,
a kind of cosmic solidarity.

'But it's still so sad,' he says. 'Think: all of us
as cut off as the living from the dead.
It's the size that's all wrong here. The emptiness.'
She says, 'Well it's a miracle I found you
in all this space and dust.' He turns his head
and smiles the smile she recognized him through.

'I wasn't saying differently. It's just –
the biggest flashlight we could put together
is a match struck in the wind out here. We're lost.'
'I only meant – there's no more we traverse
than the space between us. The sun up there's no farther.
We're each of us a separate universe.

We talk, make love, we sleep in the same bed –
but no matter what we do, you can't be me.
We only dream this place up in one head.'
'Thanks for that . . . You're saying that because
the bed's a light-year wide, or might as well be,
I'm even lonelier than I thought I was?'

'No . . . just that it's why we have this crap
of souls and gods and ghosts and afterlives.
Not to . . . *bridge eternity*. Just the gap' –
she measures it – 'from here to here.' 'Tough call.
Death or voodoo. Some alternatives.'
'There's one more. That you trust me with it *all*.'

The wind is rising slowly through the trees;
the dark comes, and the first moon shows; they turn
their lighter talk to what daft ceremonies
the people of that star – he points to ours –
might make, what songs and speeches they might learn,
how they might dress for it, their hats and flowers,

and what signs they exchange (as stars might do,
their signals meeting in the empty bands)
to say *even in this nothingness I found you;
I was lucky in the timing of my birth.*
They stare down at their own five-fingered hands
and the rings that look like nothing on that earth.

The Poetry
after Li Po

I found him wandering on the hill
one hot blue afternoon.
He looked as skinny as a nail,
as pale-skinned as the moon;

below the broad shade of his hat
his face was cut with rain.
Dear God, poor Du Fu, I thought:
It's the poetry again.

Sky Song

after Robert Desnos

The flower told the shell: *you shine*
The shell told the sea: *you echo*
The sea told the boat: *you shudder*
The boat told the fire: *you glow*

The fire said: *far less than her eyes*
The boat said: *far less than your heart*
The sea said: *far less than her name*
The shell said: *far less than your desire*

The flower turned to me and said: *she's beautiful*
I said: *Yes, she's beautiful, she's so beautiful,*
    I can hardly speak of it

March Wind

after Salvatore Quasimodo

I will know nothing of my life but its mysteries,
the dead cycles of the breath and sap.

I shall not know whom I loved, or love
now that in the random winds of March

I am nothing but my limbs. I fall
into myself, and the years numbered in me.

The thin blossom is already streaming from my boughs.
I watch the pure calm of its only flight.

The Wind
after Antonio Machado

The wind pulled up and spoke to me one day.
The jasmine on his breath took mine away.

'This perfume can be yours too, if you want:
just let me carry off your roses' scent.'

'My roses? But I have none left,' I said.
'The flowers in my garden are all dead.'

He sighed. 'Give me the fallen petals, then.
The leaves that rattle in the empty fountain.'

With that, he left me. And I fell to weeping
for the garden that they gave into my keeping.

The Landscape
after Robert Desnos

I dreamt of loving. The dream remains, but love
is no longer those lilacs and roses whose breath
filled the broad woods, where the sail of a flame
lay at the end of each arrow-straight path.

I dreamt of loving. The dream remains, but love
is no longer that storm whose white nerve sparked
the castle towers, or left the mind unrhymed,
or flared an instant, just where the road forked.

It is the star struck under my heel in the night.
It is the word no book on earth defines.
It is the foam on the wave, the cloud in the sky.

As they age, all things grow rigid and bright.
The streets fall nameless, and the knots untie.
Now, with this landscape, I fix, I shine.

The Bowl-Maker
after Cavafy

On this wine-bowl beaten from the purest silver,
made for Herakleides' white-walled home
where everything declares his perfect taste –
I've placed a flowering olive and a river,
and at its heart, a beautiful young man
who will let the water cool his naked foot
forever. O memory: I prayed to you
that I might make his face just as it was.
What a labour that turned out to be.
He fell in Lydia fifteen years ago.

Miguel

after César Vallejo

I'm sitting here on the old patio
beside your absence. It is a black well.
We'd be playing, now . . . I can hear Mama yell
'Boys! Calm *down*!' We'd laugh, and off I'd go
to hide where you'd never look – under the stairs,
in the hall, the attic . . . Then you'd do the same.
Miguel, we were too good at that game.
Everything would always end in tears.

No one was laughing that August night
you went to hide away again, so late
it was almost dawn. But now your brother's through
with this hunting and hunting and never finding you.
The shadows crowd him. Miguel, will you hurry
and show yourself? Mama will only worry.

Verse

He's three year deid, an aa I've done is greet
wi a toom pen an nae elegy but *och.*
I've jist nae hert to mak a poem o it.
I stole that line from Robert Garioch.

Phantom

i.m. M.D.

I

The night's surveillance. Its heavy breathing
even in the day it hides behind.
Enough is enough for anyone, and so
you crossed your brilliant room, threw up the shade
to catch the night pressed hard against the glass,
threw up the sash and looked it in the eye.
Yet it did not stare you out of your own mind
or roll into the room like a black fog,
but sat there at the sill's edge, patiently,
like a priest into whose hearing you confessed
every earthly thing that tortured you.
While you spoke, it reached into the room
switching off the mirrors in their frames
and undeveloping your photographs;
it gently drew a knife across the threads
that tied your keepsakes to the things they kept;
it slipped into a thousand murmuring books
and laid a black leaf next to every white;
it turned your desk-lamp off, then lower still.
Soon there was nothing in that soundless dark
but, afloat on nothing, one white cup
which somehow had escaped your inventory.
The night bent down, and as a final kindness
placed it in your hands, so you'd remember
to halt and stoop and drink when the time came
in that river whose name was now beyond you
as was, you found indifferently, your own.

II

Zurbarán's *St Francis in Meditation*
is west-lit, hooded, kneeling, tight in his frame;
his hands are joined, both in supplication
and to clasp the old skull to his breast.
This he is at pains to hold along
the knit-line of the parietal bone
the better, I would say, to feel the teeth
of the upper jaw gnaw into his sternum.
His face is tilted upwards, heavenwards,
while the skull, in turn, beholds his upturned face.
I would say that Francis' eyes are closed
but this is guesswork, since they are occluded
wholly by the shadow of his cowl,
for which we read the larger dark he claims
beyond the local evening of his cell.
But I would say the fetish-point, the *punctum*,
is not the skull, the white cup of his hands
or the frayed hole in the elbow of his robe,
but the tiny batwing of his open mouth
and its vowel, the *ah* of revelation, grief
or agony, but in this case I would say
there is something in the care of its depiction
to prove that we arrest the saint mid-speech.
I would say something had passed between
the man and his interrogated night.
I would say his words are not his words.
I would say the skull is working him.

III

(Or to put it otherwise: consider this
pinwheel of white linen, at its heart
a hollow, in the hollow a small hole.
We cannot say or see whether the hole
passes through the cloth, or if the cloth
darkens itself – by which I mean *gives rise*
to it, the black star at its heart,
and hosts it as a mere emergent trait
of its own intricate infolded structure.
Either way, towards the framing edge
something else is calling into question
the linen's own materiality
and the folds depicted are impossible.)

after Alison Watt: 'Breath'

IV

Zurbarán knew he could guarantee
at least one fainting fit at the unveiling
if he arranged the torch- or window-light
to echo what he'd painted in the frame.
This way, to those who first beheld the saint,
the light that fell on him seemed literal.
In the same way I might have you read these words
on a black moon, in a forest after midnight,
a thousand miles from anywhere your plea
for hearth or water might be understood
and have you strike one match, and then another –
not to light these rooms, or to augment
what little light they shed upon themselves
but to see the kind of dark I laid between them.

V

We come from nothing and return to it.
It lends us out to time, and when we lie
in silent contemplation of the void
they say we feel it contemplating us.
This is wrong, but who could bear the truth.
We are ourselves the void in contemplation.
We are its only nerve and hand and eye.
There is something vast and distant and enthroned
with which you are one and continuous,
staring through your mind, staring and staring
like a black sun, constant, silent, radiant
with neither love nor hate nor apathy
as we have no human name for its regard.
Your thought is the bright shadows that it makes
as it plays across the objects of the earth
or such icons of them as your mind has forged.
The book in sunlight or the tree in rain
bursts at its touch into a blaze of signs.
But when the mind rests and the dark light stills,
the tree will rise untethered to its station
between earth and heaven, the open book
turn runic and unreadable again,
and if a word then rises to our lips
we speak it on behalf of everything.

VI

For one whole year, when I lay down, the eye
looked through my mind uninterruptedly
and I knew a peace like nothing breathing should.
I was the no one that I was in the dark womb.
One night when I was lying in meditation
the I-Am-That-I-Am-Not spoke to me
in silence from its black and ashless blaze
in the voice of Michael Donaghy the poet.
It had lost his lightness and his gentleness
and took on that plain cadence he would use
when he read out from the *Iliad* or the *Táin*.

Your eye is no eye but an exit wound.
Mind has fired through you into the world
the way a hired thug might unload his gun
through the silk-lined pocket of his overcoat.
And even yet the dying world maintains
its air of near-hysteric unconcern
like a stateroom on a doomed ship, every
table, chair and trinket nailed in place
against the rising storm of its unbeing.
If only you had known the storm was you.

Once this place was wholly free of you.
Before life there was futureless event
and as the gases cooled and thinned and gathered
time had nothing to regret its passing
and everywhere lay lightly upon space

as daylight on the world's manifest.
Then matter somehow wrenched itself around
to see – or rather just in time to miss –
the infinite laws collapse, and there behold
the perfect niche that had been carved for it.

It made an eye to look at its fine home,
but there, within its home, it saw its death;
and so it made a self to look at death,
but then within the self it saw its death;
and so it made a soul to look at self,
but then within the soul it saw its death;
and so it made a god to look at soul,
and god could not see death within the soul
for god was *death. In making death its god*
the eye had lost its home in finding it.
We find this everywhere the eye appears.
Were there design, this would have been the flaw.

VII

The voice paused; and when it resumed
it had softened, and I heard the smile in it.

Donno, I can't keep this bullshit up.
I left this message planted in your head
like a letter in a book you wouldn't find
till I was long gone. Look – do this for me:
just plot a course between the Orphic oak
and fuck 'em all if they can't take a joke
and stick to it. Avoid the fancy lies
by which you would betray me worse than looking
the jerk that you're obliged to now and then.
A shame unfelt is no shame, so a man's
can't outlive him. Not that I ever worried.
Take that ancient evening, long before
my present existential disadvantage,
in Earl's Court Square with Maddy, you and Eva,
when I found those giant barcodes on the floor
and did my drunken hopscotch up and down them
while the artist watched in ashen disbelief . . .
Oh, I was always first to jump; but just because
I never got it with the gravity.
I loved the living but I hated life.
I got sick of trying to make them all forgive me
when no one found a thing to be forgiven,
sick of my knee-jerk apologies
to every lampstand that I blundered into.
Just remember these three things for me:

always take a spoon – it might rain soup;
it's as strange to be here once as to return;
and there's nothing at all between the snow and the roses.
And don't let them misread those poems of mine
as the jeux d'esprit I had to dress them as
to get them past myself. And don't let pass
talk of my saintliness, or those attempts
to praise my average musicianship
beyond its own ambitions: music for dancers.
All I wanted was to keep the drum
so tight it was lost under their feet,
the downbeat I'd invisibly increased,
my silent augmentation of the One –
the cup I'd filled brimful . . . then even above the brim!
Nor you or I could read that line aloud
and still keep it together. But that's my point:
what kind of twisted ape ends up believing
the rushlight of his little human art
truer than the great sun on his back?
I knew the game was up for me the day
I stood before my father's corpse and thought
If I can't get a poem out of this . . .
Did you think any differently with mine?

He went on with his speech, but soon the eye
had turned on him once more, and I'd no wish
to hear him take that tone with me again.
I closed my mouth and put out its dark light.
I put down Michael's skull and held my own.

[59]

Rain

I love all films that start with rain:
rain, braiding a windowpane
or darkening a hung-out dress
or streaming down her upturned face;

one big thundering downpour
right through the empty script and score
before the act, before the blame,
before the lens pulls through the frame

to where the woman sits alone
beside a silent telephone
or the dress lies ruined on the grass
or the girl walks off the overpass,

and all things flow out from that source
along their fatal watercourse.
However bad or overlong
such a film can do no wrong,

so when his native twang shows through
or when the boom dips into view
or when her speech starts to betray
its adaptation from the play,

I think to when we opened cold
on a starlit gutter, running gold
with the neon of a drugstore sign
and I'd read into its blazing line:

forget the ink, the milk, the blood –
all was washed clean with the flood
we rose up from the falling waters
the fallen rain's own sons and daughters

and none of this, none of this matters.